T0208251

A Free Mind in the City

Hajji Wali Ahmed Furqan

iUniverse, Inc.
Bloomington

A FREE MIND IN THE CITY

iUniverse books may be ordered through booksellers or by contacting:

iUniverse
1663 Liberty Drive
Bloomington, IN 47403
www.iuniverse.com
1-800-Authors (1-800-288-4677)

Because of the dynamic nature of the Internet, any web addresses or links contained in this book may have changed since publication and may no longer be valid. The views expressed in this work are solely those of the author and do not necessarily reflect the views of the publisher, and the publisher hereby disclaims any responsibility for them.

Any people depicted in stock imagery provided by Thinkstock are models, and such images are being used for illustrative purposes only.

Certain stock imagery © Thinkstock.

ISBN: 978-1-4759-8965-6 (sc)
ISBN: 978-1-4759-8964-9 (hc)
ISBN: 978-1-4759-8963-2 (ebk)

Library of Congress Control Number: 2013908756

Printed in the United States of America

iUniverse rev. date: 5/13/2013

A man cannot be free when his mind is a slave to the influences of his environment. This book is written in gratitude to those persons in our lives who have tried to help free our minds. It is dedicated to individuals who visit and live in cities around the world and have not become participants in immoral behavior or become victims of the cities' sinister influences. G-d, family, and friends: Your patience, help, and guidance have made me the person I am.

Table of Contents

Prologue   A Reflective Memory ix

Chapter 1   Are You Free Yet? 1

Chapter 2   Freedom Comes, Freedom Goes 5

Chapter 3   Freedom from the Lottery and Gambling 11

Chapter 4   The Story of the Traveling Man 17

Chapter 5   Momma Stein Was a Free Woman with a
            Free Mind 19

Chapter 6   Freedom from Excessive Material
            Possessions 25

Chapter 7   "I Wish I Knew How It Would Feel to Be
            Free" 29

Chapter 8   Freedom from a Salty Tongue 31

Chapter 9   Free from Perception: Why Do You Let Your
            Pants Sag? 39

Chapter 10 Freedom from Sex in the Inner City 43

Chapter 11 Freedom from Drugs in Your Neighborhood and the Drug Pushers..47

Chapter 12 Damaged Goods: Recognized, Repaired, and Free 55

Chapter 13 Free to Shoot or Not to Shoot 59

Chapter 14 The Would-Be Ambusher Is Ambushed........65

Chapter 15 One Step to Freedom..71

Chapter 16 A Free Mind in the Community 77

Chapter 17 Caregivers Are G-d's Helpers............................81

Chapter 18 Giving Back..83

Prologue
A Reflective Memory

IT WAS A WARM Arkansas spring day, and it had rained earlier that morning. I can recall this because of what happened to a five-year-old boy on this day. My older sister Bernice and my older brother Roosevelt were playing in the front yard of our home. Our home sat on a hill in front of a ravine, which was approximately fifty yards in front of our house. The ravine was shallow enough that when there was a heavy rain, the water would back up to the front of our house. On this particular warm summer morning, Bernice and Roosevelt had taken off their shoes, jumped into the water, and left me on the front porch of our home.

Their laughter and playfulness were too much for my young mind to handle. So I walked to the edge of the steps and jumped into the water to join in the fun and laughter. What I didn't know was that the level of the water was deeper than what I had thought, and I immediately became submerged. I remember looking up and seeing the water over my head. I can recall Bernice reaching down into the water, plucking me out, and putting me back on the porch. At the time of my water venture, Roosevelt was ten and Bernice was twelve.

Fifty years later, before Bernice died, I asked her about saving my life. She said she remembered it as though it were yesterday: She said she was glad she had acted the way she had because Roosevelt didn't notice that I had waded in and gone under.

This incident made an indelible mark on my memory bank. Since that incident, I have tried to take the opportunity to repay her for having been there for me. I have tried to play a major role in her sons' lives. God (G-d) always gives us opportunities throughout our lives to show our gratitude for his mercy and that of others. This incident taught me early in life to always be thankful for any help or mercy that G-d may extend to me through others.

One other thing it taught me was that I could not walk on water.

Chapter 1
Are You Free Yet?

HAVE YOU EVER QUESTIONED yourself about the many things that you feel obligated to do? Watching the must-see movies, buying the car that you just have to have, playing your favorite lottery numbers daily? In most of our lives, there are many frivolous and some not-so-frivolous must-dos that keep us from realizing freedom of thought and being.

Most baby boomers can remember the saying, "An apple a day will keep the doctor away." Now these same baby boomers see themselves as needing an aspirin a day to keep a heart attack away. We went from natural food products to artificial food products. We went from depending on something that was natural and good to something that our clinicians represent to us as something we must have. Have you ever given thought to the millions of people around the world who feel dependent on a little pill? They see it as a lifesaver. Your health should not be held captive to the pillbox or the latest miracle cure of the day.

Have you noticed people whose lives have become dependent on the pillbox? My sister and I went to visit our nephew in Las Vegas. We were sitting at his breakfast table when my sister produced a black leather bag. I thought she may have brought some food for her flight from Memphis to Las Vegas, but that was not the case. My sister had twelve or fourteen bottles of different prescription medicines she took daily. My sister was using the medicine to be as free as she could from the stress and anxieties in this so-called land of the free and the brave. Freedom is a constant resistance movement fought individually and collectively. The battle is not won from the outside before it is won from the inside. Are you free yet? Or do you still wish you knew what it means to be free?

Today's high-tech environment keeps the mind captivated by an ever-increasing number of mind toys. There are so many high-tech gadgets that keep the average person from having a free moment, a moment when he or she is not engaged with a mind-captivating toy. It is harder and harder to find a free mind in the city, free from all the mind grabbers that keep you from having time to contemplate something greater than just the mundane.

For the masses of people in the modern world, having a free mind can be an enviable achievement. The mind wants to be free, but we're inundated with so many modern-day mind toys that instead of seeking to be independent thinkers, we join the masses that are part and parcel of the culture. Our freedom to think and respond with sincere thought and vision is no longer evident. In many cases, our free will has been replaced by other persons' thoughts.

Our world today is in a war for the minds of the masses. The mass media, primarily the television with its hundreds of channels, can keep a person locked into forty-eight inches of platinum for hours at a time. Tony, a friend of mine, tells his wife that when he gets home from work and sits down to watch his big screen that he is not to be disturbed for anything. His wife allows him to indulge in this.

My friend Rasheed, who lives in Las Vegas, said freedom is the ability to think freely for yourself without parroting someone else's ideas. Unfortunately, that is becoming a lost art.

A lot of people follow the path of least resistance. Rather than think objectively or independently, a lot of people simply follow the pied piper. To be a person of contemplative thought is not advocated.

Chapter 2
Freedom Comes, Freedom Goes

_____

WE LIVE IN A culture that permits a person to say or do anything. This permission permeates the family and other social groups. Many children are allowed to defy their parents' wishes and are told they have the freedom to do as they please. Many young people will say that you cannot tell them what to do because their parents don't tell them what to do. We need to educate our youth about fact that the authority to demand that they follow business or social protocol is not determined by what their parents said or did or didn't say or do for them. In my many years of work in penal institutions, I've met youth who have told me that it was their parents' fault that they were incarcerated. In one particular case, a young man told me that his mother was one of the biggest antidrug advocates in his community and that he was one of the biggest drug dealers at the same time.

He said, "My mom knew I was in the game and dealing

for the green, but she never said anything. She only wanted her share, which I gave her."

Freedom comes at birth, a fresh start with excellent potential for every human. That freedom can be restricted or constricted by individual decisions or environmental restraints. Decisions made by parents or parental influence can help children to become model citizens or those with social issues society at large must address. Parental influence or guidance is necessary for the proper social development of our youth. If we want our youth to be independent thinkers who are not influenced by every rap video or advertisement, we as socially conscious parents should invite our sons and daughters to do what is right.

Freedom comes, and freedom goes. I heard an inmate recently released from a federal prison say that he realized while incarcerated that the most important thing in his life was his freedom—the freedom to come, go, and express himself without undo constraints. A mind is a terrible thing when it is not free. There is an old saying that if you free the mind, the body will follow. Take some time to relax, contemplate, and educate and let your mind become what it was meant to be: a mind growing intelligently with unlimited potential.

In my work in the city and state correctional facilities in Illinois and Missouri, I have met some outstanding individuals. Kasan (not his real name) was one of those individuals. He died while incarcerated in an Illinois state prison. Kasan helped me and another chaplain in our duties assisting inmates in religious services. In this particular institution, the warden allowed the inmates to have a picnic each spring, and the inmates could invite their families. This was an annual event in the 1990s at this prison.

I was to give the sermon one year at the picnic. I had volunteered at this prison for years, but this was my first picnic. I arrived early that Saturday morning to go through security so as not to be late for my talk. As I was in line waiting for my turn to be searched, there was a young African American female in front of me. I heard the female guard tell her, "Young lady, you cannot enter the prison without underwear." I should have taken this remark as an indication of things to come.

I gave my talk on the duty of believers to be faithful to their religious precepts. My talk lasted about forty-five minutes. After my talk, food was served, games were played, and family members were allowed to be with each other. On this day, I saw more sexual activities between the inmates and their female guests and wives than I thought that I would ever witness in a prison or public facility. Kasan also had a lady friend visiting him, but he didn't disrespect her like a lot of the other inmates did. I saw a lot of those inmates disrespecting their female guests in any way they could. Kasan stayed true to his religious concepts, and he walked his female guest around the perimeter of the grounds, holding her hand and talking. Kasan showed me, the prison guards, and other visitors at this picnic that he was free to be moral in an immoral environment.

At another state prison in Illinois, an incident happened with one of the inmates named Tony (not his real name)

Tony was on death row, and I was one of the chaplains who provided religious services for the death row inmates. Tony was being escorted to the prison medical facility. He told me that he had not felt the grass on his body in a long time and that he wanted to feel the grass on his body. So he said to the guard, "Say, Officer, please let me roll around on the grass a bit and ask those tower guards not to shoot me."

The guard did as Tony asked, and Tony rolled around for about two minutes. "It was a brief taste of freedom," he said.

Tony and I got to be good friends during his incarceration. He became an accomplished artist, and I have one of his paintings in my home. Tony and Kasan both died while they were incarcerated, but they influenced me to become a better person, and I appreciate the opportunity to have met these men, both of whom had free minds in environments that had other inmates' minds and bodies locked up.

Freedom is an inherent right given to every human being by his Creator. You lose that right only when you give up the responsibility to struggle to maintain your free mind. Any person who has the authority to lock up another human being may do so, but only you can decide to lock your own mind.

Chapter 3
Freedom from the Lottery and Gambling

FREEDOM IS A TERRIBLE thing to waste. When you choose to be a free thinker and think for yourself, you take on a tremendous responsibility to educate yourself. Most individuals don't want to take on this role. It involves time for research and observation of various issues and people. But who said having a free mind in the city is easy?

Once upon a time in our not-so-distant history, there was only one state that had legalized gambling: Nevada. In other places, public gambling and games of chance, such as the lottery, were illegal and participation in them could result in incarceration in state or federal prison.

There are many influences that rob the minds of the young and the old; these influences are gender- and race-neutral. The greatest of these influences is the opportunity to involve people in immoral activities. In my long tenure of prison ministry, I have met individuals whose personalities were identified by the city in which they committed their crimes. These individuals saw themselves as being kingpins of crime in their cities. Some of them were into the gambling racket.

Casino gambling is legal in many states today, but there are men and women who are in prison today because they played the numbers in their state before it became legal. However, making it legal has not lessened the financial and moral damage gambling can cause.

Several years ago, I was purchasing gas at a local station when I noticed that the lady in front of me had a handful of lottery cards.

"Won anything yet?" I asked her.

This was a young African American female dressed in the latest fashion apparel. She replied, "I win some; I lose some. It's my job. If I didn't play, I wouldn't have anything to do. I wouldn't have any cash either."

At some of these gas stations, I am sure there are more lottery tickets purchased than gallons of gas. In another incident, an older African American female came onto the gas station lot. The way in which she was dressed indicated that she could use a clothing overhaul. This lady was carrying a plastic bag with some aluminum cans in it; evidently, she was collecting these cans to sell. She left her cans outside the station as she went inside. (I followed her into the building.) She went to the checkout counter and gave the cashier her lottery ticket; it was a two-dollar winner.

"Give me two more one-dollar tickets," she told the cashier. Taking the tickets, she thanked the man, stuck them in her pocket, and left the station. I assume she waited until she got home to do the scratch-off.

Unfortunately, those who play the lottery and other games of chance are often the individuals who can least afford to. They give their minds over to the illusion that they are the one out of ten million who is going to win. I think this is one of the greatest marketing schemes of our day. But in African American and other poor communities throughout our land of plenty, people are forever praying to be that lucky one. "If you don't play, you can't win" is the mantra of these wizards of advertising.

The Yusef Ali edition of the Holy Quran says, "They ask you about drinking and gambling. Tell them: 'There is great sin in both, although they have some benefit for men; but their sin is greater than the benefit'" (S.XI.219).

The lottery advertising geniuses have sold the average lottery players on the idea that their odds of winning are great and that they will never have the experience of winning if they don't play. However, the odds of winning are not good. Analysts have calculated that a person is twenty thousand times more likely to be struck by lightning than to win the Mega Millions jackpot. Analysis of other games suggests that a person is one hundred times more likely to die of a flesh-eating bacteria than to win. In the $338 million New Jersey Powerball, the chances of winning were only one in

75 million. This is in contrast to one of 11.5 million people who owe back child support. Likewise, one of 12.5 million are owed back child support to the tune of a collective $100 billion.

The lottery is a fantasy drama sold to the poor and middle-class working poor who buy these drama dreams for one dollar per episode. Savvy investors who analyze the best gambling stock and invest in the stock of lottery companies make a 3 to 4 percent annual return or better and are pleased with the modest return because their principal or initial investment is secure. The consistent return and the multiplying effect on their investment will secure their future and the future of their children and grandchildren.

The poor and working poor are sold the dream of instant wealth. The reality is that to secure wealth, you must have a plan of investment by which the return on your principal is greater than the loss. A secure investment with modest, consistent returns is the prudent way to secure your financial well-being.

Here's a method of saving that was suggested to me later in life. This is only one method of saving for a special occasion. Each January, open a savings account and set aside any amount that you can save on a weekly or monthly basis without any financial difficulty. Have your employer deposit that money directly into your savings account through direct deposit at your bank or credit union. At the end of the year, you can withdraw this saved amount and use the funds to invest in something that will give you a good return on your investment, or you can use the monies for you and your family to go on a vacation. I used this method to take my family on a four-day Caribbean cruise. I had my part-time employer make direct deposits into my savings account. I would take most of the money from my part-time job and put that amount into my savings account.

The best investment I made for my family and me was my home, and the second best was to purchase some run-down investment real estate. When bought at a price you can afford, investment property can give you consistent supplemental income. I'm constantly trying to interest friends and family members in investing in properties in which other people might not want to. These properties have excellent potential investment opportunity if the buyers have sufficient funds to make the properties viable places to reside in.

The lottery and other games of chance are just another way to keep the poor dreaming of their lucky number one day becoming a reality. In reality, the best way of accumulating wealth is a plan of saving and investing at a modest and consistent rate.

Chapter 4
The Story of the Traveling Man

I AM SURE MOST of us have heard the Bible story about the prodigal son. The gist of the story is about two sons whose father is a king. One of the two sons wants to go out into the world to experience what life is like outside his father's kingdom.

The narrative states that the younger son leaves his father's kingdom, and in his travels, he has many perverse and degrading experiences. Some of his experiences are so degrading that they eventually lead him to wallow in the mud with the pigs. The son becomes tired of the degrading and humiliating experiences of travels and sends a message to his father saying that he wants to come home. His father, happy about the return of his younger son, asks his servants to prepare a feast for the homecoming of his lost son. The older son, who stayed home, asks his father why he is treating the brother with such honor when the brother disrespected him and left home while he remained, did whatever was asked of him, and was never treated with a feast.

The father replied to the faithful son who remained at home that all he has belongs to him, but that he was joyous to see the lost son return home.

This story may be interpreted in many different ways, but this is an interpretation that has meaning for my life and that I hope can be of help to others. I see this as being about the individual's life and his relationship with his Creator. There is a struggle between that inner being that wants to be guided right and that inner self that wants to experience illicit or immoral behavior. In this story, the illicit behavior is the victor for a brief period. The individual suffers because of his immoral indulgences. His soul is not at peace with its experiences and calls out to its Creator for relief from its hurt and pain. His Creator hears the desire of his soul to be free and responds to his crying soul with peace and guidance back to righteousness.

I am not saying this interpretation is definitive, but this is an interpretation that is pleasing to my spirit, and I hope it will cause us to be more reflective about this story and other scriptural narratives we read. Scripture is to be reflected on for its implicit and explicit meaning, and only G-d knows its true meaning.

Chapter 5
Momma Stein Was a Free Woman with a Free Mind

LIKE THE FATHER IN the prodigal son story, my mother never let anyone forget how important her children were to her.

My mother's daughters-in-law called her Momma Stein. We, her children, called her Momma. Our mother was the kind of woman who was liked by everyone she met. She chewed tobacco and dipped snuff (Garrett) at the same time and carried a switchblade knife with a match in it to keep the blade slightly raised for quick opening. She was small in stature, approximately four foot three, with the most gorgeous chocolate skin tone and beautiful white teeth. She was a beautiful queen to me, with shoulder-length, silky black hair, but you would be in trouble if you would let her appearance fool you.

She would get into your chest if you made her angry. I saw Momma hit one of my older brothers in the head with a cast iron skillet because he came home drunk after drinking some corn whiskey. She hit her pregnant daughter with a fire log for talking back. I was the victim of one of Momma's whippings because I didn't move fast enough when she told me to. I tried several times to act as though I was having an asthma attack, and Momma would say, "That's okay—I'll whip the breath back into you." Needless to say, that asthma attack ploy didn't work on my mother. I saw my mother put my father in a choke hold when he tried to get romantic with her while she and our father were separated. She insisted that men respect women. My brother Jerry told us of the time our mother beat her oldest son, Robert Junior, for fighting his wife. Jerry said Robert Junior's wife told Momma that Robert Junior had fought her and knocked her down and that some men had seen under her dress in the process.

Our mother found Robert Junior and asked him why he knocked his wife down and embarrassed her with men looking under her dress. Robert Junior told Momma, "Leave me alone, little woman. She is my wife, and I can do whatever I want to do with her."

Those words were a mistake. Momma only replied, "Okay."

Then she turned away from Robert Junior as if she were leaving. Robert Junior turned his head to walk away, as well. Suddenly, Momma sucker punched him in the back of his head. That sucker punch knocked him down, and Momma stomped on him as he lay on the ground, begging her to stop. Momma didn't take any stuff.

Momma grew up in a rough time and raised us under tough circumstances. Though my wife and I embrace spanking, and never from anger, we also motivate and discipline much more with hugs and positive reinforcement. We recognize that Momma was sometimes physical with her family because she loved us.

Momma told us when we were children that she could not do day work and take care of other people's children, because she had to take care of her own. Momma was her own person, and she never let you forget that.

Our mother wore khaki pants and khaki shirts most of the time because that was her customary dress for the work she did as a chopper, picker, or puller of cotton. Mother picked or pulled cotton in the fall and traveled to Florida during the off-season to harvest fruit to support her children back in Arkansas. In fact, our mother was in Florida on the eventful day my sister Bernice rescued me from drowning in our front yard. But being away did not keep her from providing for us. Momma would send money home for our oldest brother, Sonny, to buy food for us and take care of us in her absence. I don't see this as something unique to our mother, but I see this as an inherent desire in all mothers to see their children survive to the best of their abilities.

One of my sisters constantly reminds me of our mother's benevolence, and I remind her that all women, if they are true to their nature, will seek to provide for and protect their children. You see in the mother cat with her kittens and the mother duck with her ducklings the same protective concern our mother had for her young. Our mother was only following the guidance G-d put in her original nature. Our mother never showed her children anything but motherly love and respect. During our parents' separation and until our mother remarried, I never saw a man in our home for anything more than a visit. No man other than her husband ever spent the night in our home.

Momma gave me some of the best advice that I ever received. She told me when I was very young that I should learn how to read. When my mother would come home from working in the fields, she would ask my baby sister and me to wash her tired feet in Epsom salt to soothe her aching toes and soles. My baby sister and I would read the King James Version of the Bible during these foot-washing episodes.

When I was promoted to the seventh grade at Harrison High School in Blytheville, Arkansas, Ms. Robinson, our social studies teacher, told a very noisy group of seventh graders to be quiet and find something to read. Ms. Robinson was the person who would rekindle in my mind something that my mother had said to me when I was very young: "Boy, I want you to learn how to read."

Our social studies class was held in the library of Harrison High School. Ms. Robinson's words inspired me to look on the bookshelves for something to read. I picked up **The Count of Monte Cristo**, a classic by the French writer Alexander Dumas, and my love for reading was sparked forever.

However, it was my mother who planted the seed in her son's young mind to love hard work and literature and be consistent in both endeavors if I wanted to succeed in life. My mother was my first encounter with a person who had a free mind.

My mother played a significant role in my marriage. I met my wife-to-be as a sophomore at Northeast Missouri State University in Kirksville, Missouri, in 1972. I had read an article in the college paper about this young, beautiful African American math whiz who had received a scholarship to attend Northeast Missouri State University. What I noticed most about the picture was how very much the lady who would become my future wife looked like my mother.

I called my mother and told her, "I saw this woman that I will someday marry, and she looks just like you."

My mother only laughed softly and said, "Son, go ahead and marry her then."

Thirty-eight years and six children later, that lady and I are still married. My wife had a massive stroke in 2006 and suffered a significant amount of short- and long-term memory loss. I am part of my wife's caregiving team and have the assistance of an adult day care facility that she attends for eight hours a day, five days a week. Our youngest daughter and I attend to my wife when she is home in the evening. We do our best to take care of all her needs. G-d blessed our children and me with my wife's care for thirty-three years. Now it is our turn to take care of her. I pray every day that G-d will allow me to return the favor to her for the care that she gave me and our family. Our family is challenged daily with the needs of my wife, but with G-d's grace and mercy, we will be successful.

We are simply continuing the legacy of love and caring that was first modeled for us by our mothers.

Chapter 6
Freedom from Excessive Material Possessions

WE LIVE IN A culture of excess. Too much food, clothing, cars, and other personal indulgences have caused us to lose all rational decision-making ability about consumption. We live in a culture that says if one is good, ten are better. Plus, if you buy ten, you can get a 10 percent discount.

In the movie **Born Free**, the star is a lion, but the human animal is born with a free mind. A mind is subject to the environment in which it evolves. The human race is capable of making what is natural unnatural and what unnatural natural. Several years ago, when I was on a business trip to Chicago, I met a young lady who said that she didn't like water. She said that her drink of choice was orange soda. This drink was 80 percent of this young lady's liquid consumption. Because of this choice, this young lady eventually developed kidney problems. She had taken a drink that should have been a sometimes refreshment and drank it as she should have water. She was born free to choose the kind of liquid refreshment she would consume. Her natural inclination was to consume water, but her mind had been influenced to think that orange soda, because of its sugary taste, was better for her than water. Her problems with her kidneys eventually caused her to reevaluate her beverage of choice. We are all born with free minds, but because of the mind snatchers we can lose our free minds.

James, a skilled carpenter and a Vietnam veteran, told me that he was stressed when he played the lottery and was stressed when he didn't play the lottery. James played the lottery twice a day. He would purchase a morning lottery ticket, and he would purchase an afternoon lottery ticket. He would do this rain or shine, seven days a week. James had a serious gambling habit that he found stressful to live with but even more stressful to live without. James had lost his freedom to spend his money in a nonstressful way. He had lost his free mind to the mind snatchers.

A good friend of my family, whom we have known for more than thirty-five years, is a professional craftsman. His mother and father were devoutly religious people, and he is very knowledgeable about his religion. But during this entire period I have known him, he has had a problem with drugs, initially with marijuana and now with crack cocaine. This man has a strong family support system, but he has allowed his constant drug use to dominate his life. To the detriment of his marriage and profession, drugs have snatched his mind and made him a slave to their constant demand.

Our desire to have more puts us in a position of unsustainable debt. We have had personal and collective debt collapse in our economy. There are two types of debts for most households: those that can be sustained by our personal incomes and those that are unsustainable by our personal income and dependent on other resources. Excessive debt is economic slavery. It can cause severe depression and a need to rearrange basic ideas about personal consumption.

Our bankruptcy courts are filled with consumers who have been hooked on excessive purchases. Those excessive purchases caused those individuals to dig themselves further and further into unmanageable debt. This indiscretion has led most debtors straight to the steps of bankruptcy court.

My uncle Clarence once told me, "If you want to get anything, you have to go into debt to get it."

Unfortunately, my uncle never told me about the destructiveness of debt, and I allowed myself to overindulge in debt that I couldn't sustain. Soon, I too found myself on the bankruptcy court steps. So my advice to you is that if your income now and in the foreseeable future can't support your purchases, don't buy them. Wait until your finances will allow you to make the purchases without financial strain. Take it from someone who has been there and done that.

The Yusef Ali translation of the Holy Quran, says it even better (S.XVII.26–27):

And rendered to the kindred

Their due rights, as (also)

To those in want,

And to the wayfarer:

But squander not (your wealth)

In the manner of a spendthrift.

Verily spendthrifts are brothers

Of the Evil Ones;

And the Evil One

Is to his lord (Himself) Ungrateful.

Chapter 7
"I Wish I Knew How It Would Feel to Be Free"

THIS IS THE TITLE of a song by Nina Simone, who probably is best known for her song "To Be Young, Gifted, and Black." "I Wish I Knew How It Would Feel to Be Free" was also a favorite of song of Dr. Martin Luther King Jr. Whenever Ms. Simone was present at one of Dr. King's rallies, he would ask her to sing this particular song. Most people are slaves to something they wish they were free of. Their lives are directly encumbered by that lack of freedom of thought or direct action that causes their collective and individual lives not to be all that they have the potential to be. "I Wish I Knew How It Would Feel to Be Free" is a song but also a spirit that has to be fulfilled. A human being is never free when there is something burdening his or her soul. Ms. Simone's song echoed those sentiments with which Dr. King could empathize.

Dr. King expressed those sentiments in one of his

speeches when he stated, "Injustice anywhere is a threat to justice everywhere." Is there a greater injustice than a person's being unjust to themselves and others? During the 1950s, 1960s, and 1970s, freedom rallies for people of color and women's rights saturated the media. The individuals in the forefront of these movements were seeking equal justice for their causes. However, some of those same people were not treating themselves or others justly. This is what Dr. King wanted all of them to understand— justice starts at home.

There is a constant evolution toward economic, spiritual, mental, and physical freedom. In this era of instant messages via Twitter, Skype, and the like, the suppression of any of those freedoms can instantly be exposed. This is what has happened in the recent Arab Spring uprisings in the Middle East. People instantaneously shared their stories of injustice and soon gathered incredible support. Dr. King's experience foreshadowed this trend when his marches and the ensuing violence were covered extensively by national television networks. No longer was it possible to hide the injustice.

Indeed, the civil rights movement and its exposure through print and television coverage gave the world a view of the struggles of African Americans and caused a freedom movement that is still being witnessed today.

Chapter 8
Freedom from a Salty Tongue

MY BROTHER JERRY DIED in January 2011. Jerry had a tongue that I shall politely refer to as salty. In short, Jerry had a tongue that was as foul as it could be. Jerry was a heavy curser in the worst way. But if you could take his cursing, he was a good person.

If there is such a thing as inheriting a foul mouth, Jerry inherited his cursing ability from our grandmother, Grandma Mag. Our grandmother stayed at one of her daughter's homes, my mother's or her younger sister's. Our mother and her younger sister together had about twenty children, and my cousins, my siblings, and me would sometimes be left in the care of Grandma Mag. When one of the young grandchildren would act out and disturb Grandma Mag's peace, all her grandchildren would incur her wrath. Her cursing at us would be full force; she would call us names as foul as any we would ever hear. The guilty individual would also be in for a whipping, and it was up to the rest of us to bring the guilty grandchild to Grandma.

Grandma was confined to a wheelchair because she was paralyzed on her left side. The other thing that she had to keep us in control was a walking cane. After cursing us out, she would use that cane to pop us anywhere she chose to hit us. Grandma Mag was one of the influences from whom my brother Jerry learned.

The other person who influenced our brother Jerry was our Uncle Sank, our mother's brother. Obviously, Uncle Sank learned his cursing from his mother, Mag, and Uncle Sank would call us some of the foulest names.

Our grandmother, our uncle, and Jerry were all cursers extraordinaire. But they were also kindhearted people if you could get past their salty language. After Grandma Mag died, our mother left us in the care of our brothers Sonny and Jerry when she went to Florida in the winter months. Although they were very young men, Sonny and Jerry would cook and take care of the young siblings for several months until our mother would return from Florida in the spring of the year. I was never into cursing. Whenever I was cursed at, my feelings would be so hurt. Therefore, I couldn't muster the foul words to hurt someone else's feelings.

Although my brother is dead and I am free from his salty tongue, I will miss his kind heart, and we all will remember his good deeds. Everyone knew that Jerry would call you names and say foul things to and about you. At the same time, though, he would not hesitate to help you. Early in their marriage, Jerry and his wife became foster parents of two boys and a baby girl. They would eventually adopt all three of these children.

My relationship with Jerry was put on hold and strained for several months because of how he had cursed at me during a visit my wife and I made to his home in the summer of 2010. We had called him from the city park where we were visiting on a summer outing to make sure that he was at home for our visit. When we arrived at his house, a cousin was there visiting, as well. It was a warm summer evening, so we sat out on his patio to enjoy the breeze. Our conversation was light and reflective about events of years gone by. The conversation eventually got to a topic that was touchy for my brother.

I didn't think the conversation was one to become upset about—we were merely discussing how long I had known his wife. However, the length of time that I said I had known his wife and the length of time that he said I had known her were different, and that angered him. He became so irate that he began to call me all kinds of foul names, names that would cause the average man to want to fight. When a man has his wife or his significant other with him, he would like for other men to be respectful. My feeling was that if my brother was going to berate and curse me, he should at least respect my wife, and if he could not, I would not sit in his presence and allow him to curse and berate me in front of my wife. My cousin, who was present during my brother's explosive tirade, tried to intervene and pleaded for me and my wife to stay.

"Don't leave," he said. "Jerry is just being Jerry. You know how he lets his mouth get ahead of himself sometimes."

But I was too upset and offended by Jerry's abusive outburst to stay any longer. I left my brother's home, and for the next several months, I had no contact with him. I decided that my brother had said things to me that were hurtful, words that he shouldn't have said to another person for any reason. I called my family members in Arkansas and Tennessee and told them how our brother Jerry had cursed me out and berated me in front of my wife.

On one of my visits down south, I stopped in Blytheville, Arkansas, the town where we had been raised. I visited Gene, a family friend, and I told him how my brother had cursed me and berated me in front of my wife.

Using the name my family and friends affectionately call me, Gene said, "Stanger, you know how Jerry is, and you know that he is not going to change." After a pause, he stated, "Jerry won't apologize to you. You may as well forget about that."

On my drive back to St. Louis, I reflected on what our friend had said to me, and I made up my mind that I would apologize to my brother for what he had said to me. I realized that we sometimes cut off relationships with loved ones about some small indiscretion and forget about the many good things that these people have done for us in the past. We say to ourselves in our moment of anger, "I would continue this relationship **but** for that outburst he or she might have made or some other minor infraction."

That **but** can cut off relationships that may have taken years to build and cause them to become permanently destroyed. I had to reflect on all the good deeds my brother has done for me, and I came to the realization that I would not let that **but** destroy our brotherly ties.

My relationship with my brother had always been one of respect and admiration, even when he moved to St. Louis to work in construction with our mother's brother. When I moved to St. Louis, Jerry opened his home to me and supported and helped me whenever I needed his help.

When I graduated from high school in Blytheville in 1968, Mother sent me to St. Louis to live with Jerry and his wife. When I got ready to go off to college at Northeast Missouri State University in 1970, it was Jerry who drove me to college. When I got married in 1973, it was Jerry who was my best man, the only family member who was present at my wedding. And, finally, when I graduated from college in 1974, Jerry and his wife were my only family members at the graduation. So I had to reflect on the good deeds my brother has done for me and my family. My brother has always been a good uncle to our children. I decided I wouldn't let that **but** destroy our relationship.

I called my brother, and I apologized to him for him

cursing me out. He said that was okay and said, "You know how I am, and you know how I can get real loud and nasty sometimes."

After my apology, my wife, my brother Roosevelt, and I visited Jerry at his home in December 2010. We all enjoyed the time together, and we left his home feeling good to be in each other's company again. Jerry died three weeks later.

Don't let that **but** destroy your relationships with family or friends or stop you from advancing in your life. Reconcile your differences with family members and friends before that opportunity is no longer possible. The following are a few **buts** that should not stop us from achieving some degree of success in our personal lives.

A to Z of Buts:

I would

Apply for that job, but …

Buy that, but …

Go to college, but …

Drive across country, but …

Exercise more, but …

Feed myself more fresh fruit in my diet, but …

Give more to charity, but …

Help those in need, but …

Invest in real estate, but …

Join a religious organization, but …

Keep my faith in humanity, but …

Love my children's mother, but …

Marry my first love, but …

Never inhale, but …

Own up to my potential, but …

Pray more, but …

Quit smoking/drinking, but …

Ride an Amtrak passenger train, but …

Send my mother flowers, but …

Take a vacation, but …

Unite with my family, but …

Veg out on fresh vegetables, but …

Write my life story, but …

Attend Xavier College, but …

Say, "Yes, I can," but …

Plan to visit a Zoo, but …

Quite often, because of the **buts** in our lives, we experience undue frustration and miss out on many opportunities for personal growth. Pause now, and take a moment to reflect on the many **buts** in your life. Now make a concentrated effort to analyze any future **buts**, and make a vow to yourself not to allow such a small word to have such a tremendous effect on your life. Your **buts** can take your freedom to enjoy your life and even injure the relationships you have with others. No more **buts**.

Chapter 9
Free from Perception: Why Do You Let Your Pants Sag?

A FAILURE TO ACT isn't the only way we can harm our relationships. Negative or narrow perceptions can also be damaging.

Most people have subjective perceptions of other people. We should remind ourselves that someone else's perception shouldn't necessarily be our reality. Recently, I was at a friend's house when his fifteen-year-old son walked into the kitchen.

"Pull up your pants, boy," my friend said.

"Yes, sir," said the boy as he yanked up the pants.

The boy later explained that he wanted to sag his pants because "the girls like to see me sagging."

Without addressing the several analyses of the pants-sagging phenomenon, or the contradiction of trying to attract the other gender by using negative methods (for example, me as a teenager trying to look cool by smoking Kool cigarettes or females in tight, skimpy clothing displaying cleavage and other body parts that should be covered), the reality is that most boys who let their pants sag are not really gangsters. However, they must learn to stand up and have a free mind that can resist peer pressure, fads, and the impulse to attract the other gender—or be attracted **by** the other gender—with counterproductive behavior, indecent fashions, or improper conversation. Adults, on the other hand, can exhibit a free mind by being less judgmental of the youths as individuals (even while being critical of some of their actions) and teach them by setting a good example and then holding firm that they live up to our expectations of morality and responsibility.

We should realize that other people's perceptions of us don't have to be our reality. My perception of myself is my reality. We are people constantly trying to live up to other people's reality. If we are not free in our own minds, what is our true reality?

There is nothing ignorant or gangster about sagging pants. Our sons are doing some of the same things that a lot of us did when we were growing up; this is their method of attracting the attention of the young females. I am not promoting the wearing of sagging pants, but I do believe that fads come and fads go, and this one will soon pass with the aging of our sons.

All human beings in their essence have inherent nobility. The neighborhoods where they live, their formal education, the clothing they wear, or any of a number of other superficial perceptions we have of them cannot change that potential nobility.

What we perceive as our reality can be subject to our own prejudices. In the past few years, there has been a highly watched reality show on network television called **Undercover Boss**. The premise of the show is that an executive of a corporation is disguised as an ordinary employee of the company. He or she then goes to work at one of the company's business locations to experience the work ethic and job-related concerns of the firm's employees. In each episode I have seen, the undercover boss has been the big winner through his or her examination of the employees. The employees' reality surprises most owners or executives. Most bosses find that their perceptions are contrary to their employees' reality. Most bosses find employees who are dedicated to their work and their company. Most executives are moved emotionally by the real efforts and dedication of their employees.

Someone else's perception of you is not your reality. No one needs to try to act out other people's perceptions of them. In reality, there is no urban or suburban persona; the human being is too complex of an animal to be relegated to a specific region or locality. Each human is the totality of family, community, religious, and social influences.

Chapter 10
Freedom from Sex in the Inner City

ANOTHER REAL FREEDOM-ROBBING AND mind-controlling factor in our lives today is loose moral attitudes about sexuality.

Several years ago, another man and I were working in my backyard digging a ditch to replace some broken sewer lines. We had dug a trench about four feet deep, three feet wide, and eight feet long. We were busy shoveling dirt out of the trench when a young lady came into the yard where we were digging and jumped into the trench with us. She backed up to me, pulled up her pantyless dress, and told me, "Do what you want, brother. You can have me."

I told her, "Lower your dress and get out of the trench because I am not interested in having sex with you."

To be propositioned in the inner city is a routine occurrence. Recently, a friend told me that a young lady offered him a free sample of oral sex. Most of the time, sex in the inner city can be bought for a very small sum of money, which is often used to buy drugs by the person offering the cheap sex.

I was on my way to work one night, and I stopped to purchase gas. A young, well-dressed African American lady approached my truck while I was fueling my car. "Take me downtown," she said.

I told her that I was going in the opposite direction and that I was on my way to work. She pleaded and persisted in asking me, and she didn't look to be a prostitute, so I agreed to take her to where she wanted to go.

She got into my truck, and we had only driven a few blocks before she grabbed my arm and said, "I will give you a blow job for one dollar."

I pulled over and let her out of the truck, and I told her that I would not allow her to degrade herself or me.

Her appearance would have never given you the impression that she was a prostitute, but her appearance was very deceptive. I have been propositioned many times for sex in the inner city, but I thank G-d that I have never accepted an offer for sex. But, in many instances, I have taken the opportunity to try to talk to the women about their need to make better moral decisions in their lives.

Sex in the inner city has taken on a new concept; it has no connection to moral or emotional considerations. Instead, it is merely an opportunity to make a quick dollar with little effort. Some people misuse their bodies with little or no regard to the physical consequences of their actions.

Sex in the inner city has become a deadly game of chance. I refuse to participate in this game of moral decadence and invite those who invite me to do otherwise to think of the deadly consequences of their actions.

One Sunday, I was on my way home when I stopped to pick up the **St. Louis Post-Dispatch**. The **Post-Dispatch** is St. Louis's only daily newspaper, and its Sunday edition is its largest printed copy.

One of the headlines in this particular edition was about the rapid spread of AIDS in the inner-city neighborhoods of St. Louis. I pulled up to an intersection to make a left turn to go to my home. When I stopped at the intersection, a young lady called out to me to give her a ride in the opposite direction. When I told her that I was on my way home, she insisted and walked up to my car and offered to give me oral sex if I would take her to her destination.

I told her that I would not accept her offer of oral sex, but I would give her the ride because I wanted to talk with her about lifestyle. I told her to get into the car, and I would take her where she needed to go. When she got in, I asked her if she had seen the headlines in that day's **Post-Dispatch**. I told her that I had a copy in my car and that she should read the story.

She casually glanced at the headlines, and I asked what

she thought about the information presented there. I told her that she had offered to give me oral sex without any knowledge of who I was, my health status, or any questions about anything that would indicate to me that she was concerned about her health or mine. I told her that I would not degrade myself or her with her offer of oral sex and that she should be aware of the epidemic of AIDS in our community. I told her that the article in that day's paper and our meeting were not coincidental, but a clear sign from a higher power that she should be more considerate of her health.

When we arrived at her destination, she got out of my car and asked me to give her five dollars to get back to where I had picked her up. I told her to remember what we had talked about and that I had given her the ride she asked for and that was all that I was doing for her.

Sex in the inner city is cheap and dangerous. So are drugs.

Chapter 11
Freedom from Drugs in Your Neighborhood and the Drug Pushers

WHEN I MOVED TO Harper Street in the Third Ward of North St. Louis with my family in the late 1970s, drugs were not very prevalent on the streets of our neighborhood. But as crack cocaine and other drugs became popular and the babies of the late 1970s became teenagers in the 1990s, drug sales and the use of drugs became more apparent in our neighborhood.

I started buying and rehabbing properties on a two-block stretch of Harper Street in the early 1980s. The block we lived on was between Grand on the west and Glasgow on the east. I saw the real estate opportunities on our block, and I notified those home owners that if they were ever interested in selling their properties that I would like the first opportunity to buy them. The owners on the east and on the west sides of our home sold me their properties, and I rehabbed both of these properties and sold them for a very good profit.

With the funds from the sale of these properties, I set my sights on purchasing other properties on the other end of our block. There were several properties that we had an opportunity to buy. Two associates and I bought all of the available properties at the end of the block nearer to Grand Avenue.

It was decided that I would begin the rehabbing of the properties because of my carpentry skills and because our own home's proximity to the properties would help me keep them secure. Around the time I purchased these properties, several young men in the neighborhood began to take advantage of our vacant buildings. These young men would stand in front of our buildings and sell drugs. Our buildings were at the end of the block with a cul-de-sac, which gave the police only one entrance to capture the sellers. The one-way entrance allowed the sellers always to see the approaching police cars and run

We lived on the opposite end of the block; my wife would go out on our front porch and tell me whenever the young men were busy selling drugs in front of our properties. I would walk down the street to where they were selling the drugs and ask them not to sell drugs in front of our properties. I said if they would not stop, I would call the police. I told them that what they were doing was illegal and that only two things would possibly come of their illegal drug selling: jail time or death. I suggested to the young men that perhaps they could use their talents in a more legal trade and do what I was doing and buy and rehab properties.

Rather than take my advice, they continued to sell drugs on our property. I would call the police, who would respond to our call, and the young drug dealers, on seeing an approaching police car, would run in all different directions. This went on for quite some time. Eventually, the young drug dealers got tired of me calling the police. One night, they broke the windows and tore down a new deck we had built on the property they were selling drugs in front of.

Not to be defeated by these young drug dealers, I replaced the broken windows, rebuilt the deck, and kept the police informed whenever they would trespass on our property.

What eventually happened with the young men who were selling drugs in front of our buildings is the story of most drug dealers. There were three young men to whom I would speak and whom I would try to guide toward more legal means of earning a living. Two of them are dead: One was killed by a rival gang member, and the other one swallowed heroin rather than go to jail. He was jailed for a traffic violation and didn't tell the arresting officers what he had done and died in his cell from a drug overdose. The third young man's mother moved with her son out of the neighborhood.

There are three things we can do to help eliminate

the criminal elements in our neighborhoods. One, we can individually and collectively try to physically stop those persons from committing their criminal behavior in our neighborhoods. Two, we can speak directly to the persons committing crime in our neighborhoods and try to persuade them to get involved in a legal business or trade. Three, we can completely ignore these actions or abhor the actions of those persons who are involved in criminal behavior and not let them know of our displeasure. All three of these steps are acts of faith. To silently abhor those acts in our hearts and take no action is the weakest act of faith. To do nothing is equivalent to silent support.

When I initially saw the house that our family now calls home, it was a run-down, two-family duplex. There was a for-sale-by-owner sign in the broken window. The front yard was littered with used syringes, the kind used by drug addicts when they inject heroin into the veins in their arms.

In the drug world, this place was known as a shooting gallery. It was a vacant building where drugs were sold, and you could inject drugs into your arm after you bought them. I saw the potential of the building, and I also saw the opportunity to rehab the building with a minimal investment.

After several months of dedicated work, our new rehabbed home was ready for my family to move into. Upon moving into our new home, I noticed a lot of foot traffic coming and going into a house on the same block. When

I questioned the owner about the unusual amount of foot traffic going in and out of his building, he told me that he was a money lender. I told him, "I am in the real estate business, but your business looks to be yielding a better return than mine. I think I will get into your line of business."

I was only joking with him because I could guess at what was being sold from his residence since several young persons kept going back regularly to his home. He didn't laugh at my joke.

When I questioned one of the young ladies I had noticed going into this building several times about what she was buying, her response to me was, "What do you think?"

My immediate response was to talk with the owner of the building and let him know what I thought was being sold in his building and to tell him that I didn't want it to become a problem that could eventually lead to someone getting hurt. Where drugs are sold, violence has a tendency to erupt. Innocent victims are sometimes accidentally murdered in the cross fire of rival drug dealers.

I didn't want my family to be caught up in gun battles over drugs in which they were not involved or interested. I told the property owner that would create problems for him and me, and I couldn't predict my response if someone were to harm my wife or children. I suggested that maybe he could find another place for his clients could come and "borrow money." I will give G-d the credit: After our talk, that foot traffic, which was so heavy when we initially moved into our new rehabbed home, eventually stopped.

On one other occasion, I noticed a lot of vehicles stopping

in front of a building on one of the other blocks where we owned property. When I inquired about what was happening inside the building, I was told drugs were being sold there. I went home and made a flyer that stated, "The Organization of Believing Men, who fears G-d more than men, is watching for drugs being sold on this block, and we will not tolerate it."

I passed out flyers to every house that was on the three-block street, including the house where I suspected drugs were being sold.

Once again, I noticed that the vehicle traffic stopping in front of this particular building eventually came to a halt. I will give G-d the credit for taking the fear out of my heart to witness a wrong and not be afraid to speak to it. When we see something we know is wrong and that wrong will not let our souls be at peace, we should realize that G-d is the source of peace and He is always with the peacemaker. Peace is not the absence of trouble but the presence of G-d. We are never alone when we are seeking to establish peace and keep what is good in our lives or in our community. G-d will send his angels to be our helpers, and he will take the fear out of our hearts, enabling us to confront wrong wherever it is.

We should fear the displeasure of G-d, not the displeasure of other men. If G-d is pleased with us and our good deeds, all that matters in the end is G-d's judgment. To the person of little faith, one person standing up for what is right might appear to be all alone with no one to help him or her. Those of us with faith know that G-d is always with us and will never leave us alone to confront evil without his aid. With G-d's help, we have faith that the wrongdoers and evildoers will never be victorious over those of us seeking to establish what is right.

Chapter 12
Damaged Goods: Recognized, Repaired, and Free

WE MUST RECOGNIZE THE fact that as a people, African Americans are damaged spiritually, mentally, physically, and socially. We are not the only ethnic group in America to suffer from being damaged by the majority or the powers to be. We are the only group to be racially identifiable as a people, constitutionally, in a way that accorded us a status inferior to other races in America.

The first step in repairing anything damaged is the recognition of the fact that the damage has actually occurred. Without that recognition, the healing process can't begin. The people who were brought to the shores of America without their consent and told that their humanity was less than other people's must realize that other people's perceptions of them should not be their reality.

A person's reality is what G-d has given to every human being, and that is that our creation is a noble creation.

Degradation from that noble status can come from one's own hands as well as from being placed into a position of involuntary servitude to another race. Our life will always be a life of struggle and strife, but after difficulty comes ease. Man is born into toil and struggle, but after difficulties, things will surely get better. This is a promise from the Creator of the heavens and earth. Ours is a most compassionate G-d, one who rewards all righteous struggles.

The next step after recognizing that we are a people who have been damaged by others with inhuman designs on our humanity is to begin to repair our G-d-given humanity back to its rightful status as a people of noble creation. The reparation process begins with the acknowledgment of a Creator greater than his creations, one who has designed man with great potential for success or failure. Man's success or failure in life is determined by the knowledge that life's rewards are given most to those who struggle the hardest with life's obstacles and challenges. Within that struggle, we become stronger persons.

Those individuals who inflicted damage on us as a people have also suffered. Nature has a way of giving justice to those who have been treated unjustly. Among the many attributes of G-d is that He is a just G-d and that justice is always near. If we are patient, our patience will be rewarded.

The human being's essence is his or her soul. That soul is very resilient. It can be temporarily damaged or hampered, but G-d is the Creator of the soul and its final destiny is to him, to be judged for all of its good and bad deeds. The scriptures of all the major faiths constantly remind the faithful of this fact—that all of humanity came from G-d and to G-d we will return for our final judgment.

A man can damage his own soul, or some other being may seek to destroy or control his very being. Ultimately, the final domain of the soul is with its Creator. The Creator breathes into man his spirit (knowledge) and man becomes a living (knowing) soul. It is the Creator, the one who created it and gave it form, who controls everything in the heavens and earth. He has perfected his creation, and man is the highest form of that creation. Man has the ability to achieve the highest level of intellectual thought or the lowest level of animal behavior. Our omnipotent Creator has given us the ability to choose, so we must choose wisely. We pray that G-d blesses us with a sincere heart seeking G-d's pleasure in all of our righteous endeavors and that G-d blesses our sincere heart with his insight. Amen.

Chapter 13
Free to Shoot or Not to Shoot

AS WE ALL KNOW, doing the righteous act is not always easy.

In the early 1980s, I had purchased several single-family buildings, and I began to rehab them on the block where we lived. I was volunteering as a chaplain in a medium-security prison, and I would hire recently released ex-offenders to help me in my rehab projects.

At one of the buildings where we were working, we had a visitor whom I didn't want to have on my property. This person was a known thief in our neighborhood, and I was adamant about not having him stealing anything from our job site. I approached Tony (a recently released offender) and politely asked him not to come on my job site because I didn't want to have to accuse him of taking something from me. I knew that if something did come up missing, someone might get hurt. I didn't want anyone to hurt me, and I didn't want to hurt anyone, so to keep us safe from each other, I didn't want him on my job sites.

However, Tony, the neighborhood burglar, did what burglars do: He burglarized one of my job sites. I had purchased about seventeen windows. When I purchased the windows, the manufacturer put our company name, Ahad Construction, on the side of the windows.

Tony, with some assistance from someone with a pickup truck large enough to steal seventeen windows, several ladders, some saws, and other construction tools, left my building empty of any windows and construction tools. Rather stupidly, Tony tried to sell the windows to a friend of mine in the neighborhood, and this friend saw my company name on the side of the windows and called me with a good description of the person trying to sell the windows. The description fit Tony to a T.

With this information, I asked the police to arrest Tony for burglarizing my building, stealing my construction materials, and literally putting me temporarily out of business. The police told me that my accusation was not sufficient evidence to arrest someone on burglary and that I needed more evidence because I didn't have the windows.

On my way out of the police station, I told the desk sergeant, "Someone is going to kill Tony if he keeps that up."

That's where the seed was sewn for my plan to shoot

Tony for burglarizing my building. I began to immediately plot to ambush Tony and to shoot him for what he had done to me and my family. It wasn't hard to find Tony because he lived on the next street behind our house. My plan was to watch Tony from an inconspicuous place and wait until opportunity presented itself. Then, I was going to ambush him and end his burglarizing career for good.

The place I selected was a vacant house that provided me with a good view of him when he left his home and gave me good ambush cover. I watched Tony come and go from his home for several nights before I decided that I was going to shoot him for what he had done to me and my family. I had a .38 caliber pistol my brother Jerry had given me for protection. He had always been there for me when I needed his help. He said I needed a gun to protect myself when I was going in and out of all of these vacant buildings in St. Louis. But that night, my sight was set on shooting Tony.

It was about 1:30 a.m. when a car pulled up and blew its horn in front of Tony's house. I was waiting in my hiding spot to ambush Tony if he came out of his house. I pulled my gun out of its holster and had it in my hand when Tony walked out of his house to get into the car. My intention was to shoot him, but as I aimed my pistol to shoot Tony, an invisible voice spoke to me and said not to shoot him. I knew G-d was speaking to me to save me from seeking my vengeance and protecting me from my own anger.

Although I knew G-d was protecting me, I was so upset

at not shooting Tony that I began to cry and walked back to my house. It was early in the morning, and my wife and our children were all in bed. I needed something to release my tension, so I picked up the Quran to read. I knew G-d's word would provide me with the answers and the medicine for my aching soul. I opened the Quran, and this is what I read: Surah 2:109 stated that, "Many among the people of the book wish they could turn you back from belief to unbelief; due to their selfish envy, after the truth has become quite clear to them. Forgive them and bear with them until G-d brings about his command; rest assured that G-d has power over everything."

This message was soothing to my soul, and it was given to me by a merciful G-d who knew that his servant needed guidance and patience in his life.

After I realized that my vengeful thoughts and anger were something that G-d was conscious of and that his guidance was greater and more beneficial, I reflected on a hadith of our Prophet Muhammad (pbuh), in the tradition of Bukhari and Muslim: "G-d has written down the good deeds and the bad ones." Then he explained, "He who intended a good deed and has not done it, G-d writes it down with himself as a full good deed. But if has intended it and has done it, G-d writes it down with himself as from ten good deeds to seven hundred times or many times over. But if he has intended a bad deed and has not done it, G-d writes it down with himself as a full good deed."

So, amazingly, although I had intended to do a bad deed, I had not done it. G-d had now credited me with a good deed. But if a man has intended it and has done it, G-d writes it down as one bad deed. He is a most merciful and most compassionate G-d.

What I had to do now was to get back to work on my rehab project. I borrowed some necessary equipment from another contractor who was in the trade. I called on Mr. Rosenberg of Delsing Windows and Doors where I bought my windows. I explained to Mr. Rosenberg what had happened to the original order of windows and asked him if he would consign the initial order until I sold the building. Mr. Rosenberg agreed to my request, and that was the restart that I needed. The original window order was more than $3,400, and I didn't have any money after the burglary to replace the stolen materials

Some of the people we had previously helped came to my assistance in my time of need. We were able to complete the rehab project, and when we finished, the first lady who came with her Realtor agreed to purchase the building for full asking price. We were able to pay Mr. Rosenberg of Delsing Windows and other creditors who worked with us on this project. When my wife and I went to the bank to close the deal, we walked away with a good profit, grateful to G-d for his mercy and guidance.

A year later, we were informed that Tony was killed in front of his home. Coincidentally, it was the exact place where I had planned to ambush Tony.

Chapter 14
The Would-Be Ambusher Is Ambushed

A FEW YEARS LATER, the secretary of my friend Lonnie, who was a Realtor and a general contractor in home remodeling, contacted me to see if I would be interested in working on a fire-damaged residential job. I told her to tell Lonnie that I would visit the job site and let him know if the job was something we were interested in working on.

Jerry, one of our laborers, and I visited the fire-damaged property a couple of days later. He and I agreed that the project was one we could do and that it would be a profitable opportunity for the amount of work involved to restore the property back to its predamaged status. Lonnie and I agreed on a starting date and a price for the work he wanted our company to complete.

The two-story frame house had extensive damage on the first floor and in the basement. The kitchen area had suffered the most damage; it was evident that the fire had started there. There was also minor smoke damage on the second floor where the bedrooms were. We contracted to remove the fire-damaged appliances, food, clothing, and other items that could not be salvaged. We had worked on the job for approximately four days when, on a Saturday, I brought my oldest son to work with us so that he could earn some extra money for school. Matthew was fifteen and a sophomore in high school. I was busy removing some cabinets from the kitchen walls when one of the painting contractors yelled out to me that someone wanted to see me in the alley.

I had no idea who would want to see me, but I had no reason to believe that I shouldn't go and see who it was. I went out the kitchen door and made the short walk into the alley. As I approached the alley, I saw two young black men standing there. They both looked to be in their early twenties. They were about six to eight feet apart from each other and dressed in very loose-fitting clothing. The first thing that I said was, "What's up?"

The younger brother on my right side asked me, "Man, you been messing with my sister?"

I said, "Brother, my name is Wali Furqan. I am married, and I don't know what you're talking about. "

The younger brother said, "I know who you are, and you have been f--k--- with my sister."

I stated my name again, saying, "My name is Wali Furqan.

I've been married for twenty-four years. I am the father of seven children, and I don't know your sister."

About this time, I had the feeling that I had maybe put myself in a harmful situation because the young brother seemed to think that I was someone who had done some harm to his sister, and my protestations were not causing him to think otherwise. My mind immediately told me to try to calm the situation before it escalated into something deadly. I began to try to talk with the young man some more to convince him that I was not the person who had harmed his sister. As I was talking to him, I saw his right hand go into his jacket pocket and pull out a pistol.

My first reaction was to duck and run. As I was running, I heard several shots fired in my direction. I ran through the gangway between the two houses and around to the front of the house where I was working. When I got to the front, I noticed the jacket I was wearing was soaked with blood. My mind was racing, and blood was flowing from my gunshot wound. I ran to the house next to the one where I was working and knocked on the door. An elderly black lady came to the door. I told her that I had been shot and asked her to please call 911. She said she would, but she didn't ask me to come in. I walked off her porch and sat on the front steps of the house where we were working and waited for the ambulance.

It wasn't long before I heard the sirens, and I knew that at least someone would come to stop the bleeding. My son and some of the other workers came out of the house before the ambulance arrived. I told Larry Joe, one of my workers, to take my car and drive my son home and that I would talk to him later.

The EMTs arrived, put me on a gurney, and pushed me into the ambulance. On the way to the hospital, they cut the blood-soaked jacket and shirt off my body and hooked me up to an IV. I was conscious and praying all the way to the hospital. I was praying that G-d not let me die and that everything would be okay for my family and me. That ambulance rushed me to the hospital with the sirens blasting. The EMTs were preparing me so I could go immediately to the ER for an MRI upon our arrival. The MRI would detect how many times I had been shot and where the bullets were lodged.

In scripture, we are told that G-d answers every supplicant who prays to him. My prayers to G-d were that I would not die and that I would have no permanent physical damage to my body.

I was shot at several times, but the MRI indicated only one bullet, which was lodged in the muscle fibers of my left shoulder. The doctors told my wife and me that there would be more damage done by trying to remove the bullet and that it would be less harmful to leave it in. This is the type of advice given to the uninsured. I am sure if I had insurance those doctors would have tried to get as much money out of my insurance company as they could.

We have doctors, and we have the Doctor, the one G-d who created the heavens and earth and holds our lives and deaths in his hand. If it is his will, we live regardless of what the doctors say, and if it is his will, our life ends regardless of what the doctors say or do. All praises are due to G-d, and I am alive today because of his will.

Thinking back about the ambush in the alley, I never really knew why I was ambushed, but I decided to forgive and forget, although several of my friends wanted to try to find my attackers and seek revenge. But I believe that G-d is best suited for that. Also, I reflect back upon what happened to the young drug dealers who damaged my property after I had asked them not to sell drugs on my property. They were ambushed and killed, allegedly by other drug dealers. A similar incident involved Tony, who I knew broke into my building and stole all of my construction equipment and supplies. I wanted to shoot Tony, but I waited on G-d to issue his punishment or justice, and Tony was gunned down at the very place I had planned to ambush him. I am thankful to G-d that I didn't seek my revenge, but instead waited on G-d to punish Tony and those who ambushed me as he saw fit.

Chapter 15
One Step to Freedom

FOR MANY YEARS, I counseled drug and alcohol abusers on ways to maintain sobriety. They would tell me of their involvement in AA or some similar twelve-step program. I am not one to take anything from a person who believes that he or she has found something that works for him or her. The first step in the twelve-step program is the belief in a higher power. I would suggest to anyone who is serious about quitting any type of dependency that the first step from dependency, the belief in a higher power, is sufficient. There is no need for any more steps if that person has faith in quitting the addictive dependency. Scripture tells us that G-d is sufficient and will respond to all of our prayers. If we make one step to him, he will make two steps to us. If we come to him walking, he will come to us running. His help is always near, and if we pray for help with a sincere heart and have faith, our prayers will be answered. Patience is the key.

If we are sincere in our desire to become free of addiction, there is no power on earth greater than faith in G-d. One step with a sincere heart can free us from any dependence that we might have. Our faith in G-d is sufficient because G-d will reward our faith with strength on top of strength.

I recently met a lady with a gambling habit. She told me she uses any excuse to go to the casino—depression, hunger, or loneliness. Any reason will do. We become addicted to things that we hope will offer our soul some temporary relief and satisfy our desire to have peace. Drugs, gambling, and drinking may offer some temporary relief, but the pain will return when the supply of drugs, money, and alcohol is gone. Only faith in G-d with a sincere heart can bring about permanent happiness.

Drugs, alcohol, and gambling can offer some temporary relief from pain and anxiety, but if we want a permanent solution, we should take that first step and hold on to the rope of faith. The rope that G-d extends to all of us is sufficient, and it is permanent. The rope of G-d is represented by his words in scripture and those prophets or messengers that he sent to deliver his message. If we are sincere in our hearts and seek the help of G-d with a sincere heart and remember him in times of good and bad, G-d will be with us at all times to aid and assist us to overcome dependency on all false stimulants. G-d is sufficient, and everything else is insufficient. G-d is independent; everything else is dependent.

Faith is the key to freedom; faith in G-d is the key to perpetual and everlasting freedom. The human is an animal always seeking freedom. He is born spiritually free, but some of us become physical slaves to our environment. We lose that innocence of freedom we have as children. We allow our environment to control our freedom of thought and movement. Our faith is tested in our environment, and we lose the battle of faith to our environment.

The person who is dependent on artificial substances has lost the battle of faith to that substance. I am reminded of the story of a prominent rhythm-and-blues singer who told a reporter on National Public Radio how he kicked his cocaine habit. He had a prayer vigil with a minister in a storefront church. That prayer vigil restored his faith, and he has been drug-free since that meeting more than a decade ago.

I have a friend who is a pastor of a Christian church in St. Louis. He told me that at one time, he had been diagnosed with prostate cancer and that his doctor recommended chemotherapy. My friend the pastor told me that he consented to his doctor's wishes, but after several chemo treatments, he realized the treatments would not allow him to have control over his life and maintain his ministry. So he suggested to his doctor that he would stop undergoing the chemo treatments, change his diet, fast, read his Bible, and put his trust in G-d for six months. If after six months his prostate cancer was still present, he would resume chemotherapy. After six months, the doctor found that my friend's prostate cancer was in remission. The last time I talked with him, he told me that his prostate cancer has been in remission for more than ten years. Faith is the key to freedom; faith in G-d is the key to perpetual and everlasting freedom.

Faith is good medicine and has been proven in some instances to be just as effective as some prescription drugs. Science has proven that medicinal treatment and individuals with strong religious faith recover from invasive and surgical procedures faster than those individuals who don't express faith. Faith played a significant role in their recovery. Faith is a healer, and my friend in law enforcement has told me that on many occasions, his faith was more important to him than his sidearms. He told me that his faith was a protector for him when he entered dark basements and buildings, blind to what he might encounter. His faith protected him during two decades of law enforcement work. He retired from law enforcement without ever being physically harmed.

What do the blind marathoner, the person who climbs mountains while confined to a wheelchair, or the single mother (my mother) who raised a family of ten children with little or no assistance from the father of her children all have in common? All of these individuals have tapped into their faith reservoir. Faith is a gift and a trust that G-d gives every human being, and the person who realizes his or her faith potential can do extraordinary things. G-d rewards our faith in him with stronger faith, and when we witness that faith to others, the person who is the beneficiary of our witness becomes the recipient of manifested faith. We should always pray to G-d to increase our faith in him, for faith is the key to a more abundant life.

Chapter 16
A Free Mind in the Community

THE **ST. LOUIS POST-DISPATCH** did a feature story on my family in October 1993. The front-page article was titled, "Hard-Working Family Makes Good Home in a Tough Hood." The article discussed my strong desire to raise my family in a neighborhood that had become a haven for crime. Someone being shot or someone shooting at someone was a constant in our neighborhood. But I would always remind people who asked me why I lived in that environment that people make neighborhoods. If you want a safe and productive neighborhood, you should be that person who makes the difference.

One person can make a difference. I have always considered myself to be that person. When I was growing up, my mother never had her own home. We were constantly moving to different rental properties. I made a promise to myself that my family would have our own home. I was very fortunate to make a large sale at work, which was a commission-only sales job. I sold some industrial solutions on this commission-only job, and I earned more than $1,000 on one particular sale. I took my commission and used it to put a contract on our first home. It needed some upgrading, but it was an opportunity for me to give my wife something my mother never had—a home of her own.

I don't know who recommended my family for the coverage, but the word got out that there was this black urban pioneer who was trying to do some good things in a tough neighborhood. I was featured in the newspaper and on National Public Radio News. I have faith in G-d and the goodness of humanity. I believe if you do some good, you will in turn attract some good. From that initial idea to provide a home for my wife and our family, we were able to buy and rehab seven more homes on our block. We were people who had never rehabbed a property before, but with faith and a strong desire to do the right thing, we were able to make a small contribution to the betterment of the neighborhood we lived in.

I have a mantra that I often repeat to myself and of which I consistently remind others: Never be afraid to do the right thing. I firmly believe that when you commit yourself to do the right thing, you have the Creator and all of creation working along with you to complete your good deeds. Upon the completion of good deeds, we should recognize that G-d, the Creator of the heavens and the earth, is to be praised and magnified for any good we do, because all good comes from G-d.

That article got my family a tremendous amount of positive attention, and the media exposure for our business was priceless. The article highlighted the struggles of a young intercity family who was trying to balance business and family interests. At the same time, we also owned a small restaurant. My wife was the primary cook and worked along with myself and two other full-time employees. We didn't have the best of locations, and our menu of pizzas and sub sandwiches was not attractive to the neighborhood where we had the business.

Because of the lack of support for our business, my wife was overextended with the restaurant and trying to maintain our home at the same time. We decided that we should cut our losses and close the restaurant. Closing the restaurant caused us to take a substantial financial loss, but it was the right thing to do.

After we closed the restaurant, our largest income source was curtailed. I needed to find a job to fill some of that void. I was fortunate enough to find a job in the security business as a night security guard with a national security firm. The pay was not much, but along with the carpentry skills I applied during the day, the income from my security work allowed us to pay our bills and maintain most of the needs of our family.

For more than twenty years and even after the closing of our restaurant, I had volunteered in several different correctional institutions in Missouri and Illinois. My volunteer service in Illinois had put me in a situation to be offered a position as a part-time chaplain at Menard State Prison in Chester, Illinois. That position at Menard was a blessing in a time of financial need for me and my family.

I enjoyed the time I spent working at Menard, both as a state employee and as a volunteer, and I grew as a minister of the word of G-d and as a human being conscious of some of the weaknesses of man. To the men and women I met as an employee at Menard and the many inmates who allowed me to become a friend and confidant, I thank you for helping to me to become a better human being. My prayer is that G-d blesses us all to become better in our treatment and respect for the dignity of all persons in the human family.

We should always be conscious that G-d has the power to forgive over and over again and that G-d says that if we come to him with sins as big as the ocean, he is most merciful and most forgiving. G-d, whom we worship and call Lord, forgave his prophet Moses, who scripture says killed a man, and G-d forgave him and raised him to a position of honor in the brotherhood of messengers of G-d. If man wants G-d to be forgiving of him, shouldn't we be just as forgiving to each other? I pray to G-d that someday we will be.

Chapter 17
Caregivers Are G-d's Helpers

CAREGIVERS CAN BE HELPERS in many different areas. We can be caregivers for a spouse, a child, a friend, the community we live in, or the pets who love us as much as we love them. Presently, my daughter and I are caregivers to my wife. We do have some assistance from an adult day care provider, which has been the help that allows us to have a degree of flexibility in a day-to-day schedule.

"When Jesus found Unbelief on their part, He said: 'Who will be my helpers to (the work of) God?' Said the disciples: 'We are God's helpers: We believe in God, and do thou bear witness that we are Believers'" (003:052)

Chapter 18
Giving Back

IN MY BRIEF LIFE on this earth, I have had the honor to be helped and guided by many individuals who have given me words of inspiration or guided me on the path of righteousness. I would like to return that help and guidance with some of the proceeds of this book. I would hope that any help or financial assistance that we are able to generate from the sale of this book will be of some help toward their financial goals. May G-d reward our good intentions.

1. When I was a twenty-year-old new brother in the Alpha Phi Alpha college chapter here in St. Louis, I had completed two years of courses at the local community college. My hope was to complete my degree in business administration at a state college. I approached the president of our chapter and told him of my desire to continue my education and pursue my degree at a four-year school. My fraternity brother took my concern to the rest of the brothers in the

fraternity, and they gave me a $200 scholarship toward my tuition at the state college. In the 1970s, that $200 paid for almost a year's tuition. Tuition was only $125 a semester. That money was part of the funds that helped me to graduate from Truman State University (formerly Northeast Missouri State University). If we can share 10 percent of the proceeds of this book with the Scholarship Fund Drive of Alpha Phi Alpha–Epsilon Lambda Chapter, we can begin to repay that gesture of hope and brotherhood. Fraternally yours forever.

2. I have had the good pleasure to be acquainted with the founders and the directors of the Frederick Douglas Institute School and the New African Village /Hofi Ni Kwenu Academy in St. Louis for more than thirty years, Fundi Sanyika and Fundi Makini Anwisye. The Anwisyes have been devoted in their desire to instill pride in our African heritage and a strong belief in G-d as a foundation for education. They have seen the fruits of their labor in their children and the many other children who have walked through the doors of Frederick Douglas Institute. We will also make available to the Frederick Douglas Institute 10 percent of the proceeds of this book to further the financial needs of this much-needed institution in our community. May G-d continue to bless this school with all success, both now and in the future.

3. The Pioneers Culture Center in St. Louis, Missouri, is a

group of mostly older African Americans who followed the leadership of the Honorable Elijah Muhammad and his son Imam Warith Deen Muhammad. This group of older believers has taken an eyesore building and has nearly completed rehabbing it as a place of worship and community programs. What is especially outstanding is that this work has been accomplished with the limited financial resources of this elderly group of believers. We would like to provide 10 percent of the proceeds of this book to help in the continuation of programs and the remodeling of the property.

4. The Southside Wellness Center—St. Louis, Missouri. Mrs. Ollie Stewart, founder and director of the Southside Wellness Center, is an angel in our midst. G-d has blessed her to be someone to help feed the hungry and provide assistance for our older citizens. My wife is one of the clients of the Southside Wellness Center, and Mrs. Stewart treats her with the utmost care and kindness. Mrs. Stewart and her staff have provided my wife with wellness care since her stroke in 2006. I have often told Mrs. Stewart that I would be lost without the motherly concern and care that she has shown my wife and me. We would like to make available to Mrs. Stewart and the Southside Wellness center 10 percent of the proceeds of this book to spend in any manner that they choose, and

we pray that G-d continues to bless their work and their good deeds.

5. PATOY (Paying Attention to Our Youth) is a 501-c-3 not-for-profit organization dedicated to the advocacy of parental responsibility. We believe that "A Parent's Motivation is a Child's Inspiration" and that a child's aspiration is directly related to the expectations of his or her parents or guardians. We believe that most children will try to meet the expectations that are demanded of them. If we expect little and have low demands for our children, those children will meet those expectations. If we set realistic and achievable goals for our children and support them as they try to achieve those goals, most of those children will meet those goals. Those children who are high achievers have parents or significant persons in their lives who believe in their abilities and support them in their goals. We advocate that parents be responsible in being that positive and guiding force in their children's lives. We're directing 10 percent of the royalties or proceeds from the sale of this book to help and support the goals and advocacy of PATOY.

All of the aforementioned individuals and organizations have been G-d's helpers in achieving good for humanity. We pray that any assistance that we can provide in helping them is appreciated, and we are honored that we can help. We know that cities can be places that can cause undue negative influence in a person's life. The city's influence can be detrimental, both morally and spiritually, in an individual's life. We pray that those individuals who decide to become city dwellers do not become victims of the vices of the city. We pray that they become men and women whose minds are free of the decadent influences and that they become beacons of moral and spiritual strength. Amen.

As it says in the Yusef Ali Translation of the Holy Quran, The City:

> With the name of G-d, the
>
> Beneficent, the Merciful,
>
> I do call to witness This City
>
> And thou are a freeman of this city,
>
> And (the mystic ties of) Parent and Child
>
> Verily we created Man into toil and struggle
>
> Do you think that none have power over you?
>
> He may say (boastfully): Wealth have I squandered
>
> In abundance.
>
> Thinketh he that none
>
> Beholdeth to him
>
> Have we not made for him a pair of eyes?
>
> And a tongue and a pair of lips?

And shown him the two highways?

But he hath made no haste

On the path that is steep.

And what will explain

To you the path that is steep?

(It Is:) Freeing the bondman;

Or the giving of food

In a day of privation

To the orphan

With claims of relationship,

Or to the indigent

(Down) in the dust.

Then will he be

Of those who believe

And enjoin patience, (constancy,

And self-restraint), and enjoin

Deeds of kindness and compassion.

Such are Companions of the Right Hand.

But those who reject our signs, they are

The (unhappy) Companions of the Left Hand

On them will be Fire

Vaulted over (all around).

(S.XC.1-20)

About the Author

Hajji Wali Ahmed Furqan currently lives in St. Louis, Missouri, with his wife. They have seven children and two grandchildren. Wali is a graduate of Truman State University, holding a BS in business. He volunteers for the Department of Correction Prison Ministry and is the founder and president of the nonprofit group Paying Attention to Our Youth, which advocates parental responsibility.